# BRITISH RAILWAYS

# PAST and PRESENT

# No 21

## Berkshire and Hampshire

### Terry Gough

Past and Present

Past & Present Publishing Ltd

Past & Present Publishing Ltd
Unit 5
Home Farm Close
Church Street
Wadenhoe
Peterborough PE8 5TE
Tel/fax (0832) 720440

First published in June 1994

Maps drawn by Christina Siviter

British Library Cataloguing in Publication Data

A catalogue record for this book is available from the British Library

ISBN 1 85895 042 2

Printed and bound in Great Britain

WINCHFIELD: An up express from Bournemouth charges under the impressive bridge carrying only a minor road near Winchfield in August 1965. Electrification is imminent, the conductor rail already being in position on the local lines. The engine is 'Merchant Navy' Class No 35013 *Blue Funnel*.

The modern-day express is represented by a Class '442' on a Poole to Waterloo train on 22 May 1993. A second bridge has been built over the railway and this carries the M3 motorway which is in direct competition with the railway. *Both TG*

# CONTENTS

# BIBLIOGRAPHY

Around the Branch Lines, Vol 1 *by Terry Gough (OPC)*
Cross Country Routes of the Southern *by Terry Gough (OPC)*
The Didcot, Newbury & Southampton Railway *by T. B. Sands (Oakwood Press)*
Lambourn Valley Railway *by M. R. C. Price (Oakwood Press)*
Passengers No More *by G. Daniels and L. Dench (Oakwood Press)*
Rail Centres: Reading *by Lawrence Waters (Ian Allan)*

Regional History of the Railways of Great Britain, Vol 2 *by H. P. White (David and Charles)*
The Southern in Hampshire and Dorset *by Terry Gough (OPC)*
Southern Railway Halts *by R. W. Kidner (Oakwood Press)*
A Southern Region Chronology and Record *by R. H. Clarke (Oakwood Press)*
Southern Sheds in Camera *by Roger Griffiths (OPC)*
The Southern in Surrey and Berkshire *by Terry Gough (OPC)*

HAVANT: Main-line steam was rarely seen at Havant, but on 3 November 1963 Class 'U' No 31791 worked a special train and is seen approaching from the Portsmouth direction.

Nothing more interesting than a succession of BR-built electric units is normally seen at Havant, and on 21 May 1988 Class '422' No 2204 works a Portsmouth Harbour to Victoria via Hove train. More recently the monotony has been broken by the introduction of 'Wessex Electrics' on Waterloo trains and occasional 'Sprinters' on through trains from Bristol and South Wales. *Both TG*

# INTRODUCTION

T he diversity of railways within Hampshire and Berkshire makes these two counties particularly interesting to study. The London & South Western Railway (LSWR) main line from Waterloo passes through Hampshire, dividing just beyond Basingstoke for Weymouth and the West of England. The Great Western Railway (GWR) main line from Paddington cuts through Berkshire with Reading, the county town, as the first stop for many long-distance trains. Both counties also had typical country branches serving small communities. For example, in Hampshire there was a short branch to Bishops Waltham and in Berkshire a line along the Lambourn Valley.

Some lines had unusual features. The Meon Valley line linking Waterloo with Gosport via Alton was built to main-line standards, but became no more than a backwater, the alternative route through Guildford and Haslemere handling most of the Portsmouth area and Isle of Wight traffic. The Hayling Island line never pretended to be anything but a branch line, yet had an intensive service more akin to a suburban line. The Didcot, Newbury & Southampton Railway (DN&SR) line, which passed through both counties, was another oddity and only during the two World Wars did it take on any significance. Hampshire had two military railways, the more extensive being the Longmoor Military Railway.

A number of lines in both counties have been closed, some not before time, but others prematurely in view of subsequent developments. In Hampshire the major closures have been Andover to Romsey and the old route to Bournemouth, which ran from Brockenhurst via Ringwood. The Hayling Island and Bordon branches have also been closed. The Fawley branch is closed to passengers, but remains in use for oil traffic. Both military railways are completely closed. The DN&SR line and the Lambourn branch have gone, and in parts it is difficult to pick up the course of either of these railways.

On almost all lines steam was seen until at least the late 1950s. The Lambourn branch had, however, been worked mainly by GWR diesel railcars since 1937. The Portsmouth main line through Guildford was electrified before the Second World War and rarely saw passenger steam workings thereafter. The LSWR secondary routes from Waterloo to Reading and Alton were also electrified before the war, but electrification did not impinge upon other lines until 1967 when electric trains displaced steam on the Waterloo to Weymouth main line, the last steam-operated main line in the country. The Hampshire secondary routes last saw regular steam trains in 1957, when new diesel multiple units (DMUs), built at Eastleigh, were introduced. Many of the trains prior to this were worked by ex-LSWR Class 'T9' 4-4-0s and Southern Railway (SR) 'Moguls'. One branch line, that to Lymington, has been electrified.

The Western Region introduced the 'Warship' Class diesel locomotives in 1958 and the 'Western' Class in 1961, but by the mid-1970s most had been withdrawn. On secondary routes and branch lines DMUs took over from steam. In 1976 the Western Region moved away from the use of locomotives on express trains with the introduction of the high speed 'Inter-City 125' trains, a new concept in DMUs.

During the time this book was in preparation other changes were taking place in both counties, with the introduction of the second generation of BR era diesel and electric units. Bournemouth main-line services are now operated by 'Wessex Electrics', externally attractive and internally comfortable and quiet. The West of England trains are now operated by DMUs of Class '159' ('South Western Turbos'). The 'Hampshire' DMUs of the 1950s are almost extinct and their services have been taken over by 'Sprinters' and electric multiple units (EMUs), as more lines in Hampshire have been electrified. On the former GWR lines, locomotive-hauled passenger trains have been almost completely eliminated, and 'Thames Turbos' work the majority of local trains. Very few first-generation DMUs survive. The first signs of privatisation were also apparent with the provision of services on almost all ex-LSWR lines covered in this book being transferred to a shadow franchise company called 'South West Trains' from 1 April 1994.

One line is in the unique position of reverting to steam after being diesel-operated for a short while. This is the remnant of the Alton to Winchester line closed by BR and now forming the preserved Mid Hants Railway. Most trains are steam operated, with a variety of motive power including Bulleid 'Pacifics' and Maunsell 'Moguls'.

The future of the surviving railways looks bright. In the last few years several new stations have been opened, with interesting names such as Martins Heron and Hedge End. Others have been rebuilt, from major stations such as Reading to Furze Platt on the Bourne End branch. Many have been refurbished, as will be evident by studying the photographs in this book.

It has been an enjoyable experience to visit the places shown in the following pages, after a gap of about a quarter of a century. There were, however, a number of locations for which I had no material, mostly on ex-GWR lines, as a lack of resources when I was younger forced me to restrict my visits to SR territory. I am therefore pleased to acknowledge support of the several colleagues named in the captions who have kindly provided material from their collections to fill the gaps. Much of my own 1960s material was taken on the railway side of the fence, and I gratefully acknowledge the willingness of BR to allow access. The disappearance of goods yards has given closer public viewing of the railway and has meant that in most cases it has been easy to align 'past' and 'present' photographs, sometimes with the assistance of a telephoto lens. Some former stations are now privately owned and I thank those owners who allowed me on to their property. I am, as always, grateful to Derek Mercer, who has printed almost all the monochrome photographs in this book. Finally I thank my wife Cynthia who has shown understanding when I have included diversions to railway stations on what were meant to be days out together away from the everyday commitments of life.

**Terry Gough**
**Woking**

# Portsmouth main line

LIPHOOK is the first station in Hampshire on the ex-London & South Western Railway's (LSWR) Waterloo to Portsmouth line. It was one of several towns on the line served only by the slower trains, and this is the view from the down platform looking towards London in 1967.

Apart from minor items of station furniture, nothing had changed by 1992. The approaching train is the 09.20 all stations from Guildford to Portsmouth & Southsea, and is worked by Class '423' No 3490. *Both TG*

LISS station buildings were of the same style as Liphook and the outside view in 1967 shows evidence of a structural problem. The situation was obviously serious as the main building was later demolished; the current building, erected on the same site, resembles a giant greenhouse. *Both TG*

LONGMOOR MILITARY RAILWAY: Adjacent to the British Rail station at Liss was the southern terminus of the Longmoor Military Railway. A passenger service was run from here to Longmoor Downs, but was closed in the mid-1960s. Following complete closure of the railway in 1970, there were plans for the line to be sold for use by a preservation society, and during these negotiations stock was stored at Liss. The photograph shows Army Department No AD600 *Gordon*, a Ministry of Supply 0-6-0 saddle tank and two Bulleid 'Pacifics'. The Longmoor Military Railway platform is on the left.

The plans did not, however, come to fruition and the trackbed past the old station is now a public footpath. This is the view on 9 March 1993. *Both TG*

11

**LISS FOREST, LMR:** The first station out of Liss on the Longmoor Military Railway was Liss Forest, and a train is seen there in the mid-1960s hauled by Ministry of Supply 0-6-0 No 196.

There was no trace of the station during a visit in March 1993, although the position of the running lines and sidings is still easy to locate. *Both TG*

PETERSFIELD: Returning to the LSWR main line, the next station toward Portsmouth is Petersfield, junction for the Midhurst line (see 'British Railways Past and Present' No 18), which had its own platform behind the camera. Note that the loop is not electrified, and even by 1968 the goods yard had been abandoned.

The station building still stands, and the loop is now a siding. Following withdrawal of the Southern Railway electric stock (4CORs and 2BILs), all trains were worked by British Rail-built units such as 4CIGs and 4VEPs, now referred to as Classes '421' and '423' respectively. During late 1992 'Wessex Electric' units (Class '442') were introduced on the best trains of the day. On 16 October 1992 Class '442' No 2408 leaves for Portsmouth Harbour while Class '423' No 3482 enters the station on a semi-fast train bound for Waterloo. *Both TG*

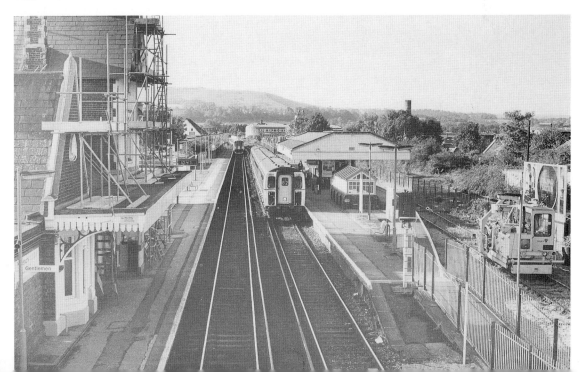

HAVANT was the junction of the Guildford line with the LB&SCR's coast line. It was also the station for the Hayling Island branch, and here Class 'A1X' No 32670 prepares to leave for Hayling Island on the morning of 22 August 1960. The main line is in the right background. The bus on the left is a foretaste of the future, as the branch bay later became a bus terminus.

However, even the bus was displaced and the branch yard is now a car park. The main station has changed little since it was rebuilt by the SR in 1938. Class '423' No 3116 leaves as an eastbound South Coast train on 21 May 1988. *Both TG*

FRATTON was separated from Havant by two halts (Bedhampton and Hilsea), and the station saw a regular steam-operated service that ran from Portsmouth & Southsea to Romsey and beyond. There were also steam and electric depots there. Fratton also saw the occasional special steam working, as for example here on 3 November 1963 when 'Battle of Britain' Class No 34088 *213 Squadron* put in an appearance.

A visit on 12 September 1993 found the scene far less interesting, with the footbridge canopy removed and most trains being worked by BR-built EMUs. The hourly service to and from Cardiff is, however, worked by Class '158' DMUs, and No 158829 from Portsmouth Harbour approaches the station on an early afternoon train. *Both TG*

PORTSMOUTH & SOUTHSEA was in effect two adjacent stations, the High Level with a through line to Portsmouth Harbour, and the Low Level terminus. The latter was used for the Salisbury and Andover Junction via Romsey steam services and slow electric services to Waterloo. In 1955 'Remembrance' Class No 32331 *Beattie* is waiting to leave on a Salisbury via Eastleigh train.

Passenger trains ceased to use this route from May 1969, and all services to Romsey and Salisbury are now routed via Southampton. Low Level station was later almost abandoned, but during rebuilding of the High Level station in 1988 Harbour station was closed and all trains terminated at Low Level. Low Level is now used regularly by slow trains to Guildford and some Southampton trains. All other trains, including those to Salisbury, start from Portsmouth Harbour. On 28 April 1993 Class '421' No 1888 leaves on the 08.29 to Southampton, while Class '158' No 158839 enters the High Level station on the 05.00 from Cardiff Central. *Peter Hay/TG*

PORTSMOUTH HARBOUR station, looking towards the Solent. Class 'L12' No 30415 is in the far easterly platform on a Salisbury via Southampton train, while to the right can just be seen a 4COR unit on a Waterloo train.

The view is remarkably similar in the spring of 1993, except that the platform is now occupied by an electric unit, No 3030 of Class '423'.
*Tony Wadmore/TG*

# Hayling Island branch

LANGSTON was the first station on the branch and was situated immediately past the main road level crossing leading to Hayling Island. With the very frequent train service on summer Saturdays, the queues of traffic on either side of the crossing meant that the train was far quicker than either the car or bus. This is Langston on 2 November 1963.

The only clue in October 1992 that there was a railway here lies in the footpath to the left of the house, which the walker will find is the former trackbed, as a notice to this effect is displayed. *Both TG*

NORTH HAYLING was an isolated and windswept station on the western edge of the island, and was smaller than many stations designated 'halts' on other parts of the Southern system. However, it had a service far more frequent than was justified by the number of passengers, and survived until the line completely closed in November 1963. Engines of Class 'A1X' were the only ones to work the line in BR days and here No 32670 enters the station from Havant on 21 August 1960.

The site of the station was easily located in 1992. The area to the left is a car park used predominantly by fishermen and walkers. *Both TG*

HAYLING ISLAND: The terminus at Hayling Island was some distance from the seafront and this was one contributing factor in the decline of the line. The crude coaling arrangement is being used on the last day of services by Class 'A1X' No 32650. The passenger facilities, to the left, consisted of just one island platform with a small booking office and waiting room. There were plans to run the line as a private enterprise, but this was abandoned in 1966.

There are now several small industrial units on the site, together with the goods shed (behind the camera), which has somehow survived demolition. This is the same location on 16 October 1992. *Both TG*

# Alton area

ALDERSHOT: The Alton line leaves the Southern's West of England main line at Pirbright Junction in Surrey, and the first station in Hampshire is Aldershot. This photograph captures a scene unchanged for decades with ex-LSWR Class '700' No 30325 shunting on 9 June 1962.

Rationalisation from the late 1960s has dramatically changed the scene. The goods yard has gone and even the bus depot which belonged to the Aldershot & District Traction Company is almost deserted. Miraculously there is still freight on the line in the form of a nightly oil train. On Saturdays this runs during daylight hours and on 31 October 1992 was hauled by Class '37' No 37220 *Westerleigh*. *Both TG*

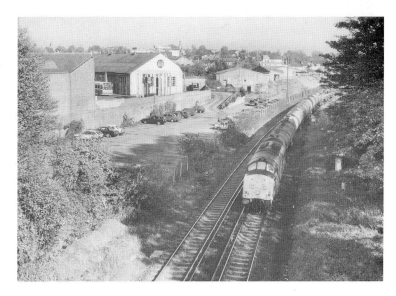

BENTLEY was the junction for the Bordon branch, which was closed to passengers in September 1957. Three years later a special train was run consisting of a push-pull unit of pre-Grouping coaches and Class 'M7' No 30028. This is the view from the up side looking toward Aldershot.

Bentley is still open for passengers and is served by Waterloo to Alton trains. The line west has been singled and the lines through the station are signalled for reversible working. Class '423' No 3405 works 'wrong line' through the station in the late afternoon of 9 March 1993. *Both TG*

BORDON was almost 5 miles south of Bentley. It served the surrounding military towns and was the interchange point for the northern terminus of the Longmoor Military Railway (LMR), which had a station adjacent to the LSWR station. Here Class 'Q1' No 33035 leaves Bordon on a special train on 14 March 1964.

Today the station area is occupied by industrial units. The only items to link the two photographs are the trees in the background and the fact that the approach road to the estate is named Station Road. Other clues, out of sight, are a row of Victorian houses and some more obvious remains of the LMR terminus. *Hugh Ballantyne/TG*

**NO 2 RANGE HALT, LMR:** The LMR saw occasional special through trains from BR, such as this train near No 2 Range Halt on 30 April 1966. The engine, Army Department No AD600 *Gordon*, had worked the train through from BR down the Portsmouth main line earlier in the day. The engine went to the Severn Valley Railway after closure of the LMR.

The land once occupied by the railway is still owned by the Ministry of Defence and is used for training purposes, as can be seen on 9 March 1993. *Both TG*

**LONGMOOR DOWNS, LMR:** A special train leaves the station in 1966 for a trip round the Hollywater Loop behind Army Department No 196. Following closure this engine was moved to the Mid Hants Railway.

The trackbed is now used for the testing of military vehicles. What was once the main station on the line just out of sight behind the rear of the train in the 'past' photograph is now part of a new section of the A3 London to Portsmouth trunk road. *Both TG*

ALTON was the end of the electrified line from Waterloo, and beyond here were steam-operated services to Winchester and Fareham. There was also a line to Basingstoke which closed in 1936. In this 1967 view a Class '73' electro-diesel locomotive shunts in the yard. Note that only one platform is served by the third rail.

Significant changes for the better have taken place at Alton, which still has a frequent electric service to London. Electric trains can now use either of the platforms in view, a crossover has been added and there is still a freight service. This train runs from Eastleigh via Woking, where it reverses; on arrival at Alton it reverses again in order to gain access to the nearby Holybourne Oil Terminal. The journey time is approximately 2½ hours; were the line to Winchester still open, the journey could be accomplished in three-quarters of an hour. On 10 March 1993 the train was worked by Class '60' No 60024 *Elizabeth Fry*. Alton is also the eastern terminus of the Mid Hants Railway, whose trains use the outer face of the island platform on the right. *Both TG*

TISTED: The steam operated line that ran from Alton to Fareham was closed as early as 1955. Class 'M7' No 30054 pauses at Tisted on 29 January, a week before closure, with the 11.56 from Fareham.

There is no difficulty in recognising Tisted in 1993. The present owners have retained a railway flavour and the buildings are in better repair than they were under BR ownership. *Both TG*

**WEST MEON, seen here 12 years after closure in 1967, deteriorated rapidly after abandonment. The station was later demolished and all that remains in 1993 are the two platforms. Trees have taken root where the buildings once stood.** *Both TG*

**DROXFORD:** There was plenty of railway-related activity here well after the closure of the station. It became the operating centre of the Sadler Railcoach Company, one of the objectives of which was to design and build a lightweight railcar for use on rural lines. Such a vehicle can be seen in the background in this 1967 view, while the diesel locomotive is hauling a Maunsell main-line coach, so common throughout the Southern Railway.

The project was abandoned in 1969 and the track was later lifted. The main station buildings remain and now form part of a private residence. *Both TG*

WICKHAM station on the occasion of a special visit by Class 'M7' No 30111 and a push-pull set on 7 March 1959. This railtour started at Portsmouth Harbour and called at several of the branch lines in southern Hampshire.

The exact site of the station is now difficult to locate. The clue is the intersection of the goods yard and running lines at the London end, and from there I was able to work backwards to identify the same spot from which the past photograph was taken. The only item of railway property in the present view is the concrete post on the left. *Both TG*

MEDSTEAD & FOUR MARKS on the Alton to Winchester line on 3 April 1966 shortly before closure. Before the advent of diesels, the normal service was operated by an 'M7' and a push-pull set. When there was engineering works between Pirbright Junction and Micheldever, Medstead saw Bulleid 'Pacifics' and heavy trains of corridor coaches *en route* for Bournemouth and Weymouth.

Following closure, everyone assumed that those days were over. But not so, as 'Pacifics' again grace the line. On 22 May 1993 'West Country' Class No 34105 *Swanage* enters Medstead & Four Marks with a Mid Hants Railway train. *Both TG*

ROPLEY, a quiet country station, is seen here on 21 September 1963. Although well kept, it had obviously seen better days, as the up platform had long since been taken out.

Dramatic changes have since taken place, with a new up platform and double track through the station. An engine shed has been built on the site of the goods yard, giving a tantalising view of both steam and diesel locomotives. The SR electric lamps have been replaced by LSWR-style 'oil' lamps. Ropley is busier than it has ever been. *Both TG*

ALRESFORD: In the last few years of BR ownership, Alton to Winchester services were operated by 'Hampshire' diesel multiple units, now Class '205'. Nos 1108 and 1121 pass at Alresford on the last day of services.

Alresford is now the administrative headquarters of the Mid Hants Railway. Diesels are still used on some trains, in this instance Class '25' No D5217 on the last train of the day in October 1992. *Both TG*

ITCHEN ABBAS was the next station towards Winchester, and in the month prior to closure DMU No 1130 calls for non-existent passengers.

All hope of reopening the line at Itchen Abbas and beyond has been extinguished, as the station site has been used for a small housing development. Two of the houses are appropriately named 'The Down Side' and 'Beeching'. *Both TG*

# South Western main line

FARNBOROUGH: Trains from Waterloo pound into Hampshire through Deepcut cutting (see 'British Railways Past and Present' No 18) before reaching Farnborough. The line here was not electrified until 1967 and apart from a very few diesel-worked trains during the transition period, all trains were steam-operated. On 16 May 1964 'Battle of Britain' Class No 34052 *Lord Dowding* stops at the station with the 14.54 Waterloo to Salisbury service.

It is now normally only the semi-fast electric trains that stop at Farnborough (now called Farnborough Main). However, during the International Air Show all express trains stop here. On 12 September 1992 Class '47' No 47707 *Holyrood* leaves on the 09.50 Waterloo to Exeter St Davids train. On the up side Class '423' No 3046 works a semi-fast Basingstoke to Waterloo train. *Both TG*

BRAMSHOT HALT was closed in 1946, but the site was easily recognisable almost 20 years later as 'Merchant Navy' Class No 35005 *Canadian Pacific* ambled past on the 14.54 semi-fast Waterloo to Basingstoke train on 27 June 1964 - something of an insult to such a powerful locomotive!

The platforms have been removed and a huge ugly pipe has been built over the railway, necessitating a high vantage point to obtain a clear view. A visit was made on 26 March 1994 to record what was advertised as the last working on the Exeter line of Class '50' locomotives. Nos 50050 and 50007 *Sir Edward Elgar* head west on a special passenger train as a 'Wessex Electric' constituting the 07.45 Poole to Waterloo train passes in the other direction. *Both TG*

WINCHFIELD: A Nine Elms to Southampton Docks freight train passes through Winchfield in July 1965 hauled by Class 'N' No 31842. The centre platforms had been abandoned many years previously and there is evident decay in the goods yard despite it still being in use.

This 1993 view shows that both the centre platforms and goods yard have finally gone, together with the signal box and imposing gantry. This was the last year of locomotive-hauled passenger trains to Salisbury and Exeter, but until delivery of the entire fleet of 'South Western Turbos' (Class '159'), all manner of odd motive power was used. On 22 May 1993 the 13.35 Waterloo to Yeovil Junction is formed of DMUs Nos 207001 and 207013 of Class '207'. *Both TG*

HOOK: Looking west from the road overbridge gives an excellent view of the railway. 'West Country' Class No 34021 *Dartmoor* approaches at speed in August 1965.

Apart from track simplification and electrification, little has changed in this 1993 view. On 22 May 'Networker' unit of Class '465', No 465237, approaches the station under test, prior to allocation to services in Kent. *Both TG*

**BASINGSTOKE (1):** A Waterloo to Bournemouth express approaches Basingstoke behind 'West Country' Class No **34009** *Lyme Regis* on 12 September 1964. To the left are the carriage sidings, while the extensive freight yards were at the country end of the station. The signals were pneumatically operated throughout their existence and were not replaced with 'colour lights' until electrification of the line.

On 26 September 1987 a special working leaves the carriage sidings behind Class '37' No 37116. Class '37s' were very unusual on the South Western main line until the spring of 1993 when several were introduced for use on the few remaining freight trains in the area. *Both TG*

BASINGSTOKE (2): At the other end of the station, a freight train for Southampton Docks passes through on the down local line on 12 April 1962 behind Class 'S15' No 30510. The rear of the motive power depot is on the left.

On 26 September 1987 Class '205' DMU No 205030 crosses from the down main to the local line after working a train from Reading. On the right is the all stations train to Bournemouth formed of a Class '423' EMU, while on the left are locomotives of Classes '73' (No 73118) and '33' (No 33027). *Both TG*

BASINGSTOKE MPD housed an interesting range of motive power on 2 September 1962, ranging from LSWR to BR steam locomotives and a diesel shunter. In the foreground are Classes '4MT' No 75077 and 'S15' No 30514.

The shed was closed in 1967, subsequently demolished and the site left derelict for many years. It is now occupied by light industrial units and offices, as seen in this photograph taken on 27 September 1992. *Both TG*

**WORTING JUNCTION** was the junction for the Bournemouth/Weymouth and Exeter lines; the up Bournemouth line was carried over the up and down Exeter lines on a flyover known as Battledown. An up vans train hauled by 'King Arthur' Class No 30782 *Sir Brian* is descending from the flyover on 12 April 1962.

On 28 May 1988 Class '50' No 50008 *Thunderer* passes with the 06.42 Exeter St Davids to Waterloo service. All locomotive-hauled trains on this line were replaced by DMUs in 1993. *Both TG*

**OAKLEY:** Several of the intermediate stations between Basingstoke and Exeter were closed during the 1960s, Oakley being one of them. Here we see the station in 1968, by this time privately owned.

Although some of the closed stations have since been reopened, Oakley remains closed. The main building is used as offices and the former goods yard is occupied by a builders merchant. Class '159' No 159007, introduced a few days previously, speeds through as the 11.50 Gillingham to Waterloo service on 22 May 1993. *Both TG*

OVERTON was the next station, serving the adjacent banknote-paper factory, as well as the nearby village. Seen here in 1967, little had changed since the day it was built.

A visit on 21 May 1993 found that the station had been completely rebuilt and the platforms lengthened in preparation for the introduction of the 'South Western Turbo' trains. The 19.51 Basingstoke to Salisbury train is formed of Class '207' No 207001. *Both TG*

WHITCHURCH NORTH consisted of one down platform and an island up platform, the north face being used as the terminating point for trains from Fullerton Junction until closure of that line in 1931 (see page 85). It was renamed plain Whitchurch following closure of the former Didcot, Newbury & Southampton Railway (DN&SR) station nearer the town (see page 138). Class '5MT' No 73088 leaves on the 07.20 Waterloo to Salisbury train in August 1964.

Several changes are evident in the spring of 1993. The station buildings on both platforms have been renovated, the main building on the down side is almost obscured by new buildings in the old yard and the up platform is no longer an island. Both platforms have been extended westward, thus giving the impression that the two photographs are taken from different points. Class '159' No 159010 enters Whitchurch forming the 18.35 Waterloo to Exeter St Davids. *Both TG*

ANDOVER JUNCTION was the meeting point of lines to Eastleigh, Southampton and the former Midland & South Western Junction Railway to Swindon and beyond; there was a bay for the Eastleigh and Southampton trains at the London end of the station on the down side. There were two small engine sheds, one Great Western and one Southern, the site of which is now occupied by the white-roofed factory in the background.

Andover formally lost its junction status in 1964, although the Swindon line is still open for MOD traffic as far as Ludgershall. An amazing sight greeted the uninformed when 'King Arthur' Class No 777 *Sir Lamiel* pulled out of Andover on a westbound special train on the morning of 18 October 1992. *Both TG*

GRATELEY is the last station on the Exeter main line in Hampshire, and was once a busy interchange for the branch services to Bulford military camp. The station had clearly seen better days and closure looked imminent when the 'past' photograph was taken in 1965.

In fact, Grateley is still open and is served by the Salisbury trains and several of those going on to Exeter. It has been refurbished since this 13 June 1987 photograph was taken and is enjoying an upsurge in passenger traffic. Class '50' No 50002 *Superb* passes through the station on the 13.10 Waterloo to Exeter. *Both TG*

# Bournemouth main line

MICHELDEVER is the first station south of Worting Junction on the Bournemouth line, and serves the nearby village and, more importantly for the railway, the adjacent oil storage depot. The extensive sidings were used to store railway stock awaiting repairs at Eastleigh or for scrap. The 'past' photograph was taken from the remains of the centre island platform that served the up and down fast lines; by this time only local trains, using the platforms on the far left and right, stopped at Micheldever. On 12 August 1961 'Merchant Navy' Class No 35021 *New Zealand Line* works the 15.30 Waterloo to Bournemouth train.

Major changes have taken place at Micheldever. The island platforms were reinstated in 1966 and there is now only one up and one down line. The old down local platform has been demolished and the up local platform is no longer used except for access to the centre platforms via a subway. Rolling-stock is no longer stored in the sidings, but there are regular oil trains. Two Class '37s' take a Freightliner to Southampton on 28 April 1993. *Both TG*

WINCHESTER CITY: When the first DMUs were introduced in Hampshire in 1957, they ran only between Southampton and Winchester City, and here we see new two-coach unit No 1109 arriving as the 12.25 from Southampton Terminus on 8 October 1957. A third coach was added to these units in 1959 and they later became designated Class '205'. Winchester City had a small engine shed to the right of the station, used for the station pilot, most unusually a Class 'P' on this occasion.

Winchester station has been refurbished and still represents an excellent example of a main-line LSWR station. On 17 March 1994 a train comprising Class '442' units with No 2410 in the lead picks up early morning passengers, mostly business men and women bound for Waterloo. *Both TG*

SHAWFORD JUNCTION: Winchester also had a station at Chesil on the DN&SR (see pages 142 and 143) and this met the LSWR at Shawford junction. The down 'Bournemouth Belle' hauled by 'Merchant Navy' Class No 35014 *Nederland Line* passes a special train hauled by Class '3MT' No 82029 on the DN&SR line on 6 September 1964.

The DN&SR has been closed for many years, although the platelayers hut has survived. The main line has become almost completely obscured. The new bridge (just visible in the distance on the left) is part of the new road system associated with the controversial extension of the M3 motorway across Twyford Down. This was under construction at the time of my visit on 18 October 1992, and further major roadworks have subsequently made the location inaccessible. *Both TG*

EASTLEIGH: The 'T9s' were displaced from Hampshire primarily as a result of the introduction of DMUs in 1957, but on 30 April 1961 No 30117 made a welcome return on a special train, seen here at Eastleigh.

In 1988, pending delivery of the 'Wessex Electric' stock, some of the Bournemouth trains were worked by electrodiesel locomotives of Class '73', the EMUs having been withdrawn. No 73119 *Kentish Mercury* pauses at Eastleigh on the 09.00 semi-fast train from Bournemouth to Waterloo on 26 March. The leading unit, No 8104 of Class '438', was one of six unpowered units formed in 1987 from trailer coaches built for the Bournemouth line in 1966. One of the original trailer units, No 8030, is on the rear of the train. *Both TG*

**EASTLEIGH LOCOMOTIVE WORKS (1):** The Works was always worth a visit, and engines awaiting scrap were a common sight. On 30 April 1961 'King Arthur' Class No 30771 *Sir Sagramore* awaits cutting up.

Defunct stock is still stored in the same area of the Works. On 27 September 1992 Class '33' No 33009 *Walrus* and a Class '423' motor coach of unit 3169 are awaiting a decision on their future. *Both TG*

EASTLEIGH LOCOMOTIVE WORKS (2): Class '0395s' were rare even as far back as the late 1950s. No 30566 was allocated to Eastleigh as the Works shunter, seen here on what is obviously an Open Day on 7 August 1957.

Another Open Day, this time 27 September 1992, finds Class '33' No 33008 *Eastleigh* in exactly the same location. In the intervening years part of the Works yard has been electrified and a new building has been constructed on the left. *Both TG*

EASTLEIGH MPD was separated from the Works by a road lined with houses built for the railwaymen. This view of 'King Arthur' Class No 30453 *King Arthur* itself and Class 'T9' No 30117 by the coaling stage on 8 July 1961 shows the Works in the background. The main running sheds were behind and to the left of the photographer.

The remains of the coaling plant embankment still existed in 1988, although the running sheds have been demolished and an electric depot built in their place. *Both TG*

SOUTHAMPTON AIRPORT: A dismal winter day sees Class '4MT' No 80033 passing the abandoned and once extensive sidings stretching south from Eastleigh. In the background is Southampton (Eastleigh) Airport, and by coincidence this photograph turned out to show the future site of Southampton Airport station, built in 1966.

The Airport station grew rapidly in importance, as a result of significantly increasing air traffic and the proximity of the M27 motorway. It was rebuilt and renamed Southampton Parkway in 1986. On 19 April 1993 Class '442' No 2401 leaves as the 14.53 Weymouth to Waterloo train. The station is also served by Intercity trains to the Midlands and the North. The different background is the result of the demolition of some of the hangers, and further changes have taken place since this photograph was taken. *Both TG*

ST DENYS is where the Bournemouth main line is joined by the line from Fareham and the South Coast. On 6 August 1958 'West Country' Class No 34039 *Boscastle* winds through the station at the head of the 11.00 Plymouth to Portsmouth and Brighton train. Bournemouth-bound trains on the main line use the right-hand face of this platform.

Less inspiring but now almost life-expired are the DMUs built for Hampshire and later the Oxted line. Class '207' No 207010 enters St Denys on 31 May 1989 forming the 13.20 Southampton to Portsmouth Harbour. This service is now operated by EMUs (see page 67). *Both TG*

**SOUTHAMPTON CENTRAL: Express departure on 5 August 1959. 'West Country' Class No 34046 *Braunton* passes the signal box with the 14.30 Waterloo to Weymouth train. The station and box were built by the SR in 1935.**

**The signal box is now closed and the station was called simply Southampton for many years until Central was added in May 1994. An Intercity train, the 09.20 York to Poole consisting of Class '253' No 253094, leaves Southampton on 19 April 1993.** *Both TG*

**MILLBROOK:** Between Southampton and Totton the line ran through an industrial area and was rather unattractive. BR Standard Class '5MT' No 73080 takes a rake of Maunsell coaches forming the 17.50 Southampton Terminus to Wimborne service on 5 August 1959. This service ran via Bournemouth, rather than the more usual route via Ringwood, and is seen west of Millbrook.

Like Southampton Airport, this location provided another co-incidence, as it was later subject to landfilling and the Southampton Maritime Container Terminal was built here. There is little to confirm that this is the same site, other than the curvature of the line, the pylons and cranes in the background and (not visible in the photograph) the mileposts. A 'Wessex Electric' unit forms an up train on 19 June 1990. *Both TG*

61

**BEAULIEU ROAD:** The scenery greatly improves after Totton as the line enters the New Forest. Lyndhurst Road and Beaulieu Road were both very attractive country stations and this photograph shows the latter on 21 September 1963.

   A visit on 18 March 1993 showed that most LSWR features had been swept away and only the station house survives. A 'Wessex Electric' unit rushes through the station as the 14.32 Waterloo to Weymouth train. *Both TG*

BROCKENHURST was the main station in the heart of the New Forest and was the junction for the Ringwood and Lymington lines, both of which were worked mostly by push-pull trains. Both lines also had some heavier trains, particularly in summer months. Here the Lymington train waits in the bay for the arrival of a London service on 7 June 1960.

The Ringwood line has been closed, but the Lymington branch is now electrified and is almost exclusively worked by a single four-coach EMU. On 21 August 1988 there was a shortage of electric units and a Class '33', No 33119, deputised, with trailer unit No 8034 of Class '438', on an evening train to Lymington. A brief return to the push-pull era. *Both TG*

NEW MILTON: 'King Arthur' Class No 30765 *Sir Gareth* passes New Milton at the head of the 11.16 Bournemouth West to Newcastle train on 28 June 1957.

Nothing significant (other than electrification) has changed at New Milton over 36 years, as the present-day shot reveals. A 'Wessex Electric' unit heads for Waterloo on the 08.53 from Weymouth on 19 April 1993. *R. C. Riley/TG*

# Southampton area

SOUTHAMPTON TERMINUS: A boat train heading for the Ocean Terminal approaches Southampton Terminus on 23 December 1965 hauled by 'West Country' Class No 34038 *Lynton*. The station closed in September 1966 but was later reopened for parcels traffic until complete closure in 1968. The Docks is reached by a line running down the side of the terminus proper.

Most of the Terminus site has been redeveloped and in 1988 the first signs of this were in evidence. Since then the view has become almost completely obscured by buildings. *Both TG*

OCEAN TERMINAL: Class 'USA' tank engines Nos 30073 and 30069 stand outside the Ocean Terminal, which was opened in July 1950; one of the 'Queens' has recently berthed. By the time this photograph was taken in 1964 new diesel locomotives built especially for the Docks had displaced most of the 'USAs'.

Well before 1993 the Ocean Terminal had been demolished, the 'Queens' had long since ceased to cross the Atlantic and the Docks had lost virtually all of its passenger traffic. All that is left of a once extensive rail network within this, the Old Docks, are a few isolated sections of track. A plaque acknowledges that the Ocean Terminal once stood here. *Both TG*

BITTERNE: The line from Southampton to Fareham passes through a heavily populated area with several closely spaced stations. After leaving the main line at St Denys (see page 58), Bitterne is the first stop. On 7 July 1957 Class '4MT' No 76063 takes a train of ex-LSWR coaches to Portsmouth & Southsea.

Although now a basic station with small waiting shelters, Bitterne still has a frequent service. On 28 April 1993 the 12.26 Southampton to Brighton train is formed of Class '421' No 1701. *Peter Hay/TG*

WOOLSTON: The 17.03 Portsmouth & Southsea to Cardiff train passes the station on 7 July 1957 behind Class 'N' No 31620.

 To this day there are still through trains to South Wales, and on 28 April 1993 Class '158' No 158863 works the 11.20 Portsmouth Harbour to Cardiff. The signal box has survived and the station is in the process of being refurbished. *Peter Hay/TG*

HAMBLE HALT was built by the SR in 1942 to serve the nearby military establishment and an oil terminal. Class '4MT' No 76065 passes through on a Southampton to Portsmouth train in July 1957.

The location is immediately recognisable. Even the oil terminal siding identified by the gate on the far left is still connected to the running lines. The only changes are of a superficial nature, apart from electrification and modern motive power. Class '158' No 158863 glides through the station as the 07.30 Cardiff to Portsmouth Harbour service in April 1993. *Peter Hay/TG*

**BURSLEDON:** Here the railway crosses the River Hamble, and 'Battle of Britain' Class No 34079 *141 Squadron* is seen on the bridge heading for Southampton in October 1964.

A 'Sprinter' is crossing the river on 31 May 1989. There was plenty of change during this period as 'Sprinters' progressively replaced the ageing 'Hampshire' DMUs. The stations on the line were in the process of being refurbished with either renovated original buildings or replacement with new waiting shelters. The line was also undergoing electrification and the third rail was in place. *Both TG*

FAREHAM, where the coast line is joined by the line from Eastleigh, was by far the most important station on the line and had extensive sidings, some of which are still used to serve an aggregates depot. On 30 April 1961 Class 'T9' No 30117 waits for the arrival of a special train, which it will then take to Southampton. In the platform is 'Hampshire' DMU No 1125 (now 205025) forming the 10.03 Portsmouth & Southsea to Salisbury.

DMUs were still in evidence in the summer of 1987. In the far platform is Class '204' No 204004 as the 16.05 Eastleigh to Portsmouth & Southsea. The nearer unit, Class '205' No 205026, operated a short-lived service which according to the public timetable ran to Templecombe; in reality the train continued to Sherborne. *Both TG*

FORT BROCKHURST: A branch that once formed the LSWR main line to Gosport ran from Fareham. There was an intermediate station at Fort Brockhurst, seen here in August 1956, three years after the withdrawal of passenger services.

The line still serves a military depot, but terminates just before Fort Brockhurst at Bedenham. The station house is in private use and the remains of the platforms are easily located among the tree beyond the house. *Both TG*

READING (SOUTHERN) MPD: 'West Country' Class No 34037 *Clovelly* graces the shed on 15 December 1963. The GW main line is on the left, and the SR terminus some distance behind the camera. The gas works is visible in the background beyond the shed.

Redevelopment of the site makes exact location of the spot difficult, but a gap in the industrial buildings that now occupy the former SR territory enables an almost matching view to be obtained. The signals controlling the WR main line and the gas holder in the background confirm the location in March 1994. *Hugh Ballantyne/Terry Gough*

SOUTHCOTE JUNCTION, just south of Reading West, is readily accessible by a public footpath that gives good views of trains on both the Basingstoke and Newbury lines. On 4 July 1959 'Castle' Class No 7022 *Hereford Castle* approaches the junction (the line on the right is not the Basingstoke line, but a spur to Central Goods).

The Central Goods line has been taken up, but the other two lines are still heavily used by both passenger and freight trains. On 17 March 1994 Class '59' No 59001 *Yeoman Endeavour* takes an empty stone train back to Merehead Quarry. *R. C. Riley/Terry Gough*

NEWBURY EAST JUNCTION was the point where the Didcot, Newbury & Southampton line from Didcot met the GWR main line between Newbury and Newbury Racecourse stations. On 7 July 1956 Class 'T9' No 30289 brings the 15.40 Didcot to Southampton Terminus train round to the junction.

There is no trace of the junction in this 1994 view, but the houses in the background act as a marker. 'Thames Turbo' No 166206 forms the 13.31 Paddington to Bedwyn train on 10 March. *R. C. Riley/Terry Gough*

HUNGERFORD: Excellent views of the railway could be obtained from Hungerford Common. On 4 July 1959 'The Royal Duchy' heads for Cornwall behind 'Hall' Class No 5976 *Achwicke Hall*.

Nature has since blocked the view, even in winter when this photograph was taken, and now it is only possible to get a glance of trains from the other side of the line. The view from the bridge in the background is also still clear, and photographs from there are included on page 122 of 'BR Past and Present' No 21. *R. C. Riley/ Terry Gough*

BASINGSTOKE (1): 'Warship' Class diesel-hydraulic locomotives were used on the South Western main line to Exeter following the end of steam. No D801 *Vanguard* waits to leave Basingstoke with a down train on 1 April 1967.

Almost 27 years later to the day at the same spot Class '442' 'Wessex Electric' No 2418 forms the 11.48 from Waterloo to Poole. The water crane, already superfluous in the 'past' photograph, has been removed. *Neil Davenport/Terry Gough*

BASINGSTOKE (2): Following the closure of the Somerset & Dorset line, the 'Pines Express' was routed via Basingstoke and Reading, and is seen at the former place bound for Manchester on 1 August 1964. The locomotive is 'Merchant Navy' Class No 35005 *Canadian Pacific*.

There are now many more workings from the South of England to the North, and even in winter there is a bi-hourly service through Basingstoke. On 17 March 1994 an 'InterCity 125' waits for a door to be closed before heading for Edinburgh as the 11.20 from Bournemouth. *Neil Davenport/Terry Gough*

WINCHESTER CITY: The road overbridge at the south end of the station gave an excellent view of the railway. On 24 June 1957 Class 'M7' No 30376 heads towards Southampton Terminus with a local train.

A visit in the winter is now necessary to obtain a clear view of the station, and this was the scene in early 1994. The platforms have been lengthened and both platelayers huts have gone as a 'Wessex Electric' pulls out of the station forming the 08.05 Waterloo to Poole train. *R. C. Riley/Terry Gough*

EASTLEIGH: A view known to thousands of railway enthusiasts - this is Eastleigh seen from the road overbridge that led to the Works and engine sheds; the Carriage & Wagon Works is in the right background. 'West Country' Class No 34012 *Launceston* works the 08.30 from Waterloo to Bournemouth on 30 August 1965.

There is now far less traffic than in steam days, but Eastleigh is still a very interesting place to visit. In mid-March 1994 'Wessex Electric' No 2417 forms the 09.48 Waterloo to Poole train. *Hugh Ballantyne/Terry Gough*

**GOSPORT: Special passenger trains were occasionally run to Gosport, such as this railway enthusiasts' train worked by Class 'M7' No 30111 on 7 March 1959.**

The line closed completely in 1969, and although the all-over roof and the track have gone, the main buildings, albeit in an advanced state of decay, still stand in 1993. *Both TG*

**BOTLEY:** Another view of the same special train between Fareham and Eastleigh. The branch to Bishops Waltham passed under the bridge in the right background.

74

Botley is still an attractive station, complete with LSWR signal box and waiting shelter on the Fareham-bound side. On the Eastleigh side the main building has given way to the usual small shelter. A roadstone depot has been built at the Eastleigh end of the station and sees several trains per week. Class '204' No 204002 forms the 16.00 Reading to Portsmouth Harbour train on 27 May 1987; the line was electrified in 1990. *Both TG*

BISHOPS WALTHAM, looking north towards an almost empty yard on 12 August 1961. Passenger services were withdrawn in 1933, but freight continued until 1962.

The station area looks at first sight to be overgrown, but in fact immediately beyond the gates is a large roundabout at the intersection of two B roads, one using the trackbed for a short distance. The trackbed going south is now a footpath for about a mile and a half. *Both TG*

**HYTHE: The Fawley branch leaves the Bournemouth main line at Totton a few miles west of Southampton and runs parallel to Southampton Water. It was built by the SR and has always had a sparse passenger service, its primary function being to serve an oil refinery. Stations were of a basic nature, such as Hythe illustrated here, where Class 'M7' No 30378 is taking water on the afternoon Fawley-bound train on 6 August 1958.**

The line was closed to passengers in 1966 and Hythe station has fallen into disrepair. However, several oil trains per day still pass the station and one such train is just discernable beyond the giant weed on the platform. At Fawley itself, where the station was within the refinery, the station buildings have been demolished, but the platform still exists. Photography is not permitted for security reasons. *Both TG*

ROMSEY (1): The station on 8 October 1957, with two-coach DMU No 1105 on the 14.03 Portsmouth to Salisbury via Southampton service. Until closure of Chandlers Ford station, passenger services were also run via Eastleigh. This route is now used only by freight trains.

On 18 March 1993 a very different DMU stands in the station. This is Class '158' No 158820 forming the 08.18 Portsmouth Harbour to Cardiff train. Romsey has remained remarkably intact and the buildings are still almost exclusively of LSWR origin. *Both TG*

**ROMSEY (2):** The same is true outside the station. These two views from the approach road would be difficult to date, were it not for the 1990s car. Ignore this and time has stood still. Perhaps even the Morris Traveller has remained in the same place for the last three decades. . . *Both TG*

**KIMBRIDGE JUNCTION:** Travelling north-west from Romsey, the line diverged at Kimbridge Junction for Salisbury and Andover Junction. A special train hauled by Class '4MT' No 82029 is seen coming off the Andover line on the last day of services, 6 September 1964.

The site of the junction on 18 October 1992 shows the 13.10 Portsmouth Harbour to Cardiff train worked by Class '158' No 158823. Although very much overgrown in the intervening years, the course of the line to Andover is still evident in many places. The farm buildings seen in the 'past' photograph still stand, hidden from view by the trees. *Both TG*

MOTTISFONT: 'Hampshire' DMU No 1130 works the 11.30 Andover Junction to Portsmouth; even on this, the last day of passenger services, little interest was shown in the railway, as can be seen by the absence of either passengers or bystanders on the platforms.

A visit on 18 October 1992 found the station building in use as a private house and a garden laid out where once was the track and platforms. *Both TG*

**Opposite page** HORSEBRIDGE (1): A visit to the station several months after closure found it still intact, if a little overgrown. The whole line remained in this state for many months before finally being dismantled during 1968 and 1969.

Horsebridge was later sold and the new owners have retained much of the railway atmosphere. An LSWR-designed corridor coach stands in the platform and a signal box and signals have been added. Although not of LSWR origin, they contribute greatly to the scene. *Both TG*

**This page** HORSEBRIDGE (2): I have visited the station on many occasions and these three photographs show the view from the Andover end of the station when the line was open, during dismantling and at the present day. The river bridge remains and forms part of a footpath; the road bridge in the background, while still in existence, is more difficult to see as the cutting has been filled in. *All TG*

STOCKBRIDGE: 'Right away' for an Andover to Portsmouth train in the spring of 1964. The line had become run down and most buildings had not been painted or repaired for many years.

There is now no trace of the station, or indeed the railway, in the Stockbridge area. All has disappeared under a road improvement scheme, which involved construction of a roundabout and road on the station site. This is a slightly more distant view, but in the same direction as the past photograph. *Both TG*

FULLERTON JUNCTION: Nowhere was more decrepit on this line (and indeed on the whole of the SR) than Fullerton Junction. Although this photograph was taken about a year after closure, the front section of canopy on the Romsey-bound platform had been in this state for decades. From here another line ran north-east to the West of England main line at Hurstbourne. Despite grand plans, it was nothing more than a country branch line and lost its passenger service in 1931.

The station buildings were surely early candidates for demolition, but to my surprise some have been used as part of what are now private houses. This is the same location (from a higher angle) in 1992. *Both TG*

**ANDOVER TOWN was also a scruffy station, even before boarding up and removal of the track. It is seen here in 1966.**

Road development makes location of the site very difficult. Part of the railway towards Andover Junction has been used for a new road and in the vicinity of the station a roundabout has been built. This is the present view; it shows no clues that it is the correct location, but behind the hedge on the right is the remains of the Romsey-bound platform, including part of the wooden waiting shelter. *Both TG*

**DUNBRIDGE is the only station in Hampshire on the Salisbury line beyond Kimbridge Junction. This is the view looking towards Salisbury in 1968. This was an attractive country station in good repair, in contrast to the stations on the Andover line.**

**The main building has been sold and is now in private use. The signal box, traditional crossing gates and signals have all been replaced, but the location remains unspoilt. Class '205' No 205032 enters the station forming the 08.40 Salisbury to Portsmouth Harbour train on 12 August 1989. Trains now only stop during peak periods, despite an attempt by BR to upgrade the importance of the station by renaming it Mottisfont Dunbridge in 1988.** *Both TG*

**AMPRESS WORKS HALT:** Further into the New Forest is the Lymington branch (see also page 63). Following closure of Shirley Holmes Halt at the turn of the century, the branch had only two stations, both in Lymington. In 1958 Ampress Works Halt was opened to serve an adjacent factory; in common with Shirley Holmes Halt it never appeared in public timetables. On 7 June 1960 Class 'Q' No 30548 passes the halt with a Brockenhurst-bound freight train.

The factory is now closed, the halt abandoned and the platform inaccessible. A slightly different viewpoint, but still looking towards Lymington, catches EMU Class '421' No 1877 without a headcode on an afternoon train to Brockenhurst on 18 March 1993. *Both TG*

**LYMINGTON TOWN: Class 'M7' No 30125 on the 16.18 Lymington Pier to Brockenhurst train pulls away from Town station on 7 June 1960. Trains were frequent and often full to capacity with passengers from the Isle of Wight ferry.**

**The once attractive view has been ruined by modern developments, with a warehouse in place of the goods yard and buses on the left where once stood the engine shed. During March 1993 all trains terminated at Town station, due to extensive repairs to the line towards the harbour. This is unit No 1877 again.** *Both TG*

HOLMSLEY, on the Ringwood line, was another attractive location. Class 'M7' No 30060 propels its train, the 10.32 from Poole, toward Brockenhurst on 7 June 1960. The coaches forming Set No 385 are converted from main-line stock.

The line closed completely in May 1964 and the trackbed has become a road. The former station house now serves teas. *Both TG*

RINGWOOD enjoyed a rare treat on 18 April 1964 when the 16.34 Bournemouth West to Brockenhurst train was worked by rebuilt 'West Country' Class No 34045 *Ottery St Mary*, instead of the expected push-pull train.

The station has disappeared under industrial development and there are few indications of its location. The only evidence to link the two photographs is the tree on the far right-hand side. At the other end of the site there is still evidence of the level crossing. The names of new roads, such as Pullman Way, also suggest that there was once a railway serving the town. *Both TG*

**FORDINGBRIDGE** lay on the Salisbury to Bournemouth line, and is seen here shortly before closure in 1964. The station was conveniently located within easy walking distance of the town centre.

Again it is the trees in the background that confirm that the location is the same as in the 'past' photograph. The road bridge is just visible, but the station buildings have been replaced by warehouses. There is still a coal yard (behind the camera), located on the trackbed, rather than its former location within the goods yard. *Both TG*

**BRAEMORE: A special train is seen heading south through the station on 18 April 1964, hauled by Class 'Q' No 30548.**

   The line closed three weeks later, but there is still much evidence of the railway. Braemore station still exists, and this 'present' view shows the road overbridge and the houses to the right of the railway. *Both TG*

# Secondary lines to Reading

**WINDSOR & ETON RIVERSIDE:** The branch for Windsor left the Waterloo to Reading line at Staines in Middlesex and terminated here in Berkshire. This photograph, taken on 26 February 1972, shows that some simplification of the layout has already taken place, with the former yard on the right being abandoned. The Waterloo service is in the hands of EPB stock.

Passenger facilities were later also reduced and an office block stands on the north side of the terminus, as seen on 17 March 1994. Trains are now worked mainly by EMUs of Class '455'. *Alan Jackson/TG*

ASCOT is also in Berkshire and is the junction on the Waterloo to Reading line for Guildford. On 19 May 1962 Class 'N' No 31858 hauls a solitary SR brake-van into the station from Guildford.

Despite track simplification and loss of some platforms, Ascot is still an interesting place to visit, particularly on race days when special trains are run from various parts of the country. On 30 October 1992 Sandite unit No 930015 leaves for Reading. These coaches were formerly from a 4EPB unit built in 1953. *Both TG*

MARTINS HERON: In the days when Feltham and Nine Elms yards were open there was a succession of freight trains to Reading and thence on to the WR. On a misty November morning in 1963 Class 'S15' No 30837 works a freight from Feltham near Ascot.

During 1988 a new station, known as Martins Heron, was opened between Ascot and Sunningdale. By pure chance the 'past' photograph was taken close to the site of the new station, which is seen here on 23 March 1993. *Both TG*

CROWTHORNE: On 25 May 1963 Class 'U' No 31624 leaves Crowthorne on the ex-SE&CR Reading to Redhill line with the 12.05 from Reading. The train consists of narrow-bodied Maunsell coaches built for the Hastings line.

As at so many stations the yard has been sold and is used in this instance by a plant hire company. No L594, a 'Cross Country' unit of Class '119', works the 10.33 Reading to Gatwick Airport service on 30 September 1992. *Both TG*

WOKINGHAM is where the South Eastern and South Western lines to Reading converge. On 6 June 1964 Class 'S15' No 30824 passes the 13.35 Redhill to Reading train, behind Class 'N' No 31408. The junction signals can be seen in the background.

On 17 May 1993 the 15.36 Guildford to Reading service is worked by Class '101' DMU No L831, recently transferred from Cambridge. Class '165' 'Turbos' progressively replaced first generation DMUs from winter 1993 on this route. The station has been rebuilt and there is an additional overbridge between the two platforms. The footbridge in the background is for public access across the railway when the level crossing barriers are closed. *Edwin Wilmshurst/TG*

**WINNERSH HALT on 29 May 1965 sees a pair of two-car SR electric units forming the 14.54 Waterloo to Reading train. The units are 2BILs, Nos 2027 and 2048.**

New facilities have been provided at Winnersh and on 23 March 1993 Class '117' DMU No L410 pulls away from the station on the 15.10 Reading to Redhill train. This is the first Redhill train of the day to stop at Winnersh - only the Waterloo trains normally stop here. *Michael Mensing/TG*

**READING (SOUTHERN) (1):** The SR terminus at Reading was known as Reading Southern and later Reading South. The approach as seen from a train window shows the almost empty motive power depot and derelict yard towards the end of the steam era. The embankment to the right carries the WR main line from Paddington.

The whole area occupied by the SR has been redeveloped and this is the site once occupied by the locomotive yard, as seen on 24 March 1993. *Ray Ruffell/TG*

**READING (SOUTHERN) (2):** On 24 October 1964 Class 'U' No 31639 acts as station pilot.

The SR station closed in September 1965, and all SR trains now use new bay platforms at Reading WR, the platform canopies of which can be glimpsed on the right. The other clue to the location is the distant clocktower of the Western Region station. There is no indication that there ever was a second station here. *Hugh Ballantyne/TG*

**BRAMLEY MILITARY RAILWAY:** Just south of Bramley station on the GWR Basingstoke to Reading line was a large goods yard for the nearby military establishment, which had its own railway. Seen on the Bramley Military Railway in 1971 is a Ruston Hornsby 0-6-0 diesel locomotive with an SR brake-van and former London Underground coaches.

The military depot was closed in 1987 and its railway abandoned. There is little evidence in this photograph to show where the railway once ran, although much of the track in the goods yard, which is to the right and out of sight, is still in place. There are proposals to use the site as a transport museum. *Both TG*

**MORTIMER on 27 November 1976 sees Class '52' No 1010 *Western Campaigner* working a special train towards Basingstoke.**

**The station is still open and an unnumbered first-generation DMU forms the 11.50 Reading to Basingstoke train. Almost all services had been taken over by 'Thames Turbos' at the beginning of the 1993 summer service, a week earlier.** *David Canning/TG*

READING WEST is seen here in the 1960s; the train in the right background beyond Oxford Road Junction is heading for Reading General, the WR main-line station, while the line to the left joins the main line west of General. The motive power depot is situated in the triangle so formed. Just south of the station, at Southcote Junction, the Basingstoke and Berks & Hants lines meet.

Today a new DMU depot occupies the vee of Oxford Road Junction. Class '243' No 243066 passes through Reading West forming the 14.35 Paddington to Penzance train on 21 June 1993. *R. C. Riley/TG*

# Lines from Paddington

**WINDSOR & ETON CENTRAL:** Changes in county boundaries have brought some former Buckinghamshire stations into Berkshire, including Slough on the GWR main line (see 'British Railways Past and Present' No 13). From here there is a short branch to Windsor, where the terminus was a large and imposing building and had a frequent service. On 18 July 1955 Class '6100' No 6143 works the branch train.

The line is still open, but there is now only one shortened platform in use. A hairdresser still occupies the same position and has acquired a new entrance to his salon. Boutiques and other tourist attractions are also to be found on the forecourt. In the background is the 'Royalty and Empire' exhibition centre, and beyond that is a large car park under the protection of an all-over roof, once part of the railway. *Alan Jackson/TG*

MAIDENHEAD has always been in Berkshire, and a down freight approaches on 26 March 1959 hauled by Class '5700' No 3697 of Slough shed. The up and down fast lines are on the far right.

Freight now is mainly in the form of oil, stone and Freightliners. I was waiting for one of the afternoon empty stone trains on 24 March 1994 when a single-car DMU came hurtling along the main line towards Reading. It was identified as Class '121' No L128 (977860), which is used as a route-learning and Sandite vehicle. *Andrew C. Ingram/TG*

**FURZE PLATT:** From Maidenhead there was a line to High Wycombe, which was closed beyond Bourne End in 1970. The first and only station on this line in Berkshire was Cookham, but a halt was built at Furze Platt, seen here looking towards High Wycombe on 28 October 1966.

Furze Platt is still open, and a train is seen approaching on the morning of 20 April 1993 consisting of Class '101' DMU No L200. *Alan Jackson/TG*

TWYFORD is the next main-line station, and the several road overbridges near the station give excellent views of the railway. In the 'past' view down trains on both the fast and local lines are seen just east of the station in the late 1950s. The train on the right is hauled by 'Hall' Class No 4948 *Northwick Hall*.

The modern scene is captured on 22 June 1993, with an 'Intercity 125' forming the 07.00 from Bristol Temple Meads heading for Paddington. In the distance a 'Thames Turbo' approaches on the local line. *Brian Morrison/TG*

**READING GENERAL (1):** A heavy freight train from the SR makes an impressive sight approaching Reading behind Class 'N' No 31809 in January 1963. The WR General station is behind the camera and the SR station to the right.

   The same location is now much tidier but less interesting. The Brighton to Preston mail train behind Class '47' No 47600 approaches Reading on the afternoon of 23 March 1993. The electrified lines on the far right are for the SR trains to Waterloo, and are also used by the Redhill and Gatwick DMU trains. *Chris Gammell/TG*

READING GENERAL (2): An up freight train passes through the station in dismal weather on 12 January 1953, hauled by 'Dukedog' Class No 9015.

On 24 March 1993 significant changes are apparent in both motive power and the station buildings. Class '243' No 243194 enters Reading on the 06.42 Milford Haven to Paddington service. The station has been rebuilt and a footbridge added; the original main buildings on the down side have been retained, but are no longer part of the station. The clocktower of the main building is illustrated on page 101. *R. C. Riley/TG*

READING (WR) MPD had an allocation of about 100 steam locomotives in early BR days. By the time this photograph was taken in 1964 the number of steam engines had dropped to 15, as diesel locomotives increasingly took over.

These in turn have been almost completely displaced by DMUs and this is the same location in April 1993. The MPD has been replaced by what is referred to as the Reading Turbo Maintenance Depot. Even first-generation DMUs are outnumbered by the recently introduced 'Thames Turbos'. The units are, from left to right, Nos L594, 165104, Departmental DMUs 97775/6 (the ATP Test Development & Training Unit), 165107 and 165101. *Philip J. Kelley/TG*

TILEHURST is the first station west of Reading on the WR main line. In the 1960s, BR Standards of the 'Britannia' Class were used on many of the expresses from South Wales, and here is No 70025 *Western Star* on the 'Red Dragon' on 17 September 1955.

Tilehurst has changed little and on 24 March 1993 'Thames Turbo' No 165106 passes the same point on the 09.15 Oxford to Paddington fast train. All stopping trains at Tilehurst use the up and down platforms on the far right. *R. C. Riley/TG*

PANGBOURNE: An inter-regional train from the North East to Bournemouth approaches Pangbourne on 17 September 1955 hauled by 'King Arthur' Class No 30742 *Camelot*. An express passenger train code is displayed, but not a Southern Region code with which the locomotive would be more familiar.

The modern scene is represented by an 'Intercity 125' and 'Thames Turbo' on the morning of 24 March 1993. The main-line train is the 06.32 Swansea to Paddington and the local train (No 165119) the 08.03 Oxford to Reading. *R. C. Riley/TG*

114

GORING WATER TROUGHS represent the last point of interest on the main line before it leaves Berkshire. A down freight train hauled by Class '2800' No 2898 is seen there in the early 1960s.

The troughs have been removed, but the scene has otherwise hardly changed over the decades. On 21 May 1993 'Thames Turbo' No 165127 heads for Oxford on the 14.07 from Paddington. *Hugh Ballantyne/TG*

THEALE is the first station on the Berks & Hants line beyond Southcote Junction. From the junction to the boundary with Wiltshire, the railway, the A4 trunk road and the Kennet & Avon Canal run in parallel. Here a 'Western' Class diesel hydraulic locomotive speeds through Theale with a passenger train bound for Paddington in 1969.

In May 1993 an 'Intercity 125' passes through the station forming the 09.42 Penzance to Paddington service. The footbridge has not only been renewed but also relocated adjacent to the road bridge. *David Canning/TG*

**ALDERMASTON** was the scene of track relaying on 23 March 1975. The diesel shunter is Ruston & Hornsby No PWM 653, now Class '97/6' No 97653.

In 1993 'Thames Turbo' No 165110 arrives on the 12.27 stopping train from Newbury to Paddington. *David Canning/TG*

MIDGHAM: A down ballast train worked by Class '52' No 1059 *Western Enterprise* approaches the level crossing in 1969.

On 21 May 1993 the modern image is represented by an empty stone train from Acton returning to Merehead Quarry hauled by Foster Yeoman Class '59' No 59005 *Kenneth J. Painter*, and seen from the other side of the line. The notices in the two photographs both warn against trespassing, the present one being much more economical with its wording! *David Canning/TG*

**THATCHAM is seen first in the 1950s, surrounded by particularly ugly industrial development.**
  There is little improvement in 1993, although the modern station buildings are in much better condition than the old GWR buildings. An 'Intercity 125' passes through with the 16.35 Paddington to Plymouth train. *Stewart Wise/TG*

NEWBURY RACECOURSE was only normally opened on race days, when a succession of special trains would arrive. 'Castle' Class No 5074 *Hampden* passes 'King' Class No 6010 *King Charles I*, both on 1st Class-only Members' race trains on 5 March 1960.

In recent years small industrial units have been built on the up side adjacent to the station. Since 1990 the station has been open experimentally on a regular basis with a service every other hour on weekdays, and all passenger trains now use the platforms on the far left. On 12 March 1993 an 'Intercity 125' forms the up 'Cornish Riviera' express. *R. C. Riley/TG*

NEWBURY station, in the centre of the town, was the junction for the Lambourn branch (which closed on 4 January 1960) and the former Didcot, Newbury & Southampton Railway (DN&SR) lines. On 7 July 1956 'Hall' Class No 6910 *Gossington Hall* heads west with a troop train, while an ex-GWR railcar can just be glimpsed beneath the platform canopy on the left, forming the Lambourn train.

Newbury has lost the up and down bays and the signal box, but the main station buildings have been retained. On 12 March 1993 Class '165' No 165115 forms the 11.50 Paddington to Bedwyn. *R. C. Riley/TG*

HUNGERFORD (1): The railway and canal are very close together between Kintbury and Hungerford, as can be seen in this photograph at Hungerford Common. 'Warship' Class No D809 *Champion* works the 16.30 Paddington to Plymouth and Kingswear train on 29 May 1965.

On 10 March 1994 an empty ARC stone train hauled by Class '59' No 59102 *Village of Chantry* makes an impressive sight as it heads west past the same point. *Michael Mensing/TG*

HUNGERFORD (2): The station is host to Class '52' No 1057 *Western Chieftain* on a westbound train in 1970. There is little evidence of much local traffic, as the car park is almost deserted.

The view in 1993 makes an interesting contrast, with 'Thames Turbo' No 165122 entering the rebuilt station on the evening of 21 May 1993. The unit is working the 17.43 from Reading to Bedwyn, the latter being the next station, which is in Wiltshire. Hungerford is now regarded as part of the commuter area, as indicated by the significant number of cars outside the station. *David Canning/TG*

# Lambourn branch

STOCKCROSS & BAGNOR HALT: River, road and railway ran in parallel along the Lambourn Valley, and numerous halts and small stations served the villages along the branch. This is Stockcross & Bagnor Halt, 2½ miles from Newbury, looking towards Lambourn in late 1959.

The line is now difficult to locate and all that remains are the abutments of what was once a railway bridge over a narrow lane. It is this that confirms the identity of the two locations. The waiting shelter, however, has survived and is now located at the Great Western Society's Centre at Didcot. *Chris Gammell/TG*

BOXFORD was another rudimentary station. A train bound for Lambourn is about to leave in this December 1959 view.
  The station approach road still exists and is now used as the private drive to a house. The station was located in the garden and this is the present-day matching view, identified by the older houses in the background (and by the owner of the house). From here too the waiting shelter has survived and in a much modified form serves as the village bus shelter. *Chris Gammell/TG*

WELFORD PARK: An unrealistic air of activity is generated by two engines at Welford Park on 19 September 1959. This location achieved some importance in the 1950s when a line was built from here to a nearby United States military establishment, which was used until 1972. Class '5700' No 7708 arrives with the 17.20 from Newbury, whither Class '2251' No 2252 is returning light engine.

The station has been demolished, but the platforms are clearly visible in 1993. The booking office exists at the Great Western Society's Centre at Didcot. *Hugh Ballantyne/TG*

**GREAT SHEFFORD, where there are parcels and Lyons cakes but no passengers in the winter of 1959.**
It is hard to detect that there was ever a railway here. Part of the station site is occupied by new houses, and beyond them are fields, as shown in this 1993 view. The curve of the field and the trees across the background are the only identifying features. *Chris Gammell/TG*

EASTBURY was another basic halt serving the adjacent village and nearby farms. This view is looking towards Lambourn.

   The footpath along the side of the railway is still in use and the other marker to link the two views is the house below the embankment. *Chris Gammell/TG*

LAMBOURN: Unlike many branch-line termini, Lambourn station was conveniently situated on the edge of the town. Class '5700' No 7788 with a single coach train waits to leave for Newbury on 1 February 1958.

The same view in 1993 is readily identified by the hut behind the water crane at the buffer-stop end of the station. The yard is occupied by industrial buildings and a house has been erected in the field beyond the station. *Chris Gammell/TG*

# Didcot, Newbury & Southampton line

HAMPSTEAD NORRIS is seen here in the summer of 1962. The station was approached by a short steep hill to the left where the chimneys of old house can be seen. A road passes under the railway at the far end of the station.

The line north of Newbury closed to passengers on 10 September 1962 and to freight two years later. A visit in the spring of 1993 revealed that the area has completely changed; there is now no trace of the station, and the overbridge and part of the embankment have been removed. This is the view from Station Hill, and today houses, behind the camera, occupy the station site. The house in the centre of the photograph is approximately in the position of the starting signal in the distance in the 'past' photograph, and the embankment, which is still in place behind this house, is at the first floor level. *Chris Gammell/TG*

PINEWOOD HALT is seen here on 16 December 1961 looking towards Didcot.
The bridge still exists, but the trackbed in the immediate vicinity has been used to dump surplus earth. Beyond this pile the land has been cleared and has been laid out as a public park. *Edwin Wilmshurst/TG*

HERMITAGE was only three-quarters of a mile south of Pinewood Halt, and was the last station before the DN&SR line met the GW main line between Newbury and Racecourse stations. Hermitage is seen here on 23 July 1962, with a single-car DMU on an afternoon train from Didcot. Towards the end of the line's life there were only four trains per day in each direction.

Like many of the DN&SR stations, Hermitage is now a private house. The trackbed immediately to the south of the station has disappeared under a field. *Chris Gammell/TG*

WOODHAY was the first station on the DN&SR south of Newbury, and is seen here on 12 December 1959 looking towards Newbury. The passenger service was withdrawn three months later. The DN&SR line was of strategic importance during both World Wars; in 1942 it was doubled from Newbury to Woodhay, and passing loops at other stations were lengthened.

The line south of Newbury closed completely on the last day of 1962, and the site of Woodhay station is now abandoned; although the platforms are still in place, the embankment and bridge at the north end of the station have been removed. *Chris Gammell/TG*

**HIGHCLERE** was typical of the stations on this line, with an attractive main building and small goods yard, as can be seen in this February 1960 view, looking south. There was, however, potential for confusion as the nearest village was Burghclere, rather than Highclere. The station is today in private ownership and stands in extensive and most attractive grounds. *Chris Gammell/TG*

BURGHCLERE itself is seen here, looking towards Newbury in February 1958. A Southampton train has just departed, from which only one passenger has disembarked. The station served the hamlet of Old Burghclere and the timetable noted that this was the alighting point for Kingsclere.

The old goods yard behind the camera is still in use by a coal merchant and the station building was under renovation at the time of my visit in March 1993. *Chris Gammell/TG*

LITCHFIELD looked forlorn even before closure, having already lost the Newbury-bound line in this 12 December 1959 view. The signal box in the background was built during the Second World War to assist in coping with the large number of additional freight trains between the Midlands and Southampton Docks. Similar ugly signal boxes were built at some of the other stations.

The A34 trunk road parallels the railway from just south of Burghclere almost to Winchester, and this has resulted in the removal of the embankment in some places. It has also made the task of identifying some locations difficult and Litchfield is an example. The station now finds itself almost buried behind earthworks resulting from construction of the upgraded A34 road, which is in a cutting immediately to the left of the camera. *Chris Gammell/TG*

WHITCHURCH TOWN was also photographed in December 1959. Another lightly patronised station, a sole passenger leaves the station with his own local means of transport. The LSWR main-line station of Whitchurch (by this time called Whitchurch North) was about 1¼ miles away.

This is yet another DN&SR station that has survived into the 1990s as a private house. A public footpath runs parallel to what was the trackbed, while the A34 road, which used to pass through the town to the east of the line, now runs to the west of the old station. *Chris Gammell/TG*

SUTTON SCOTNEY was at the intersection of the A34 and A30 trunk roads and the station was situated just to the south of this point. Here it is, again in December 1959, with a Southampton-bound train attracting a little revenue from the local post office.

The buildings have gone and an office block has been erected on the site, but part of the platforms are still in existence and the yard is used by Associated Asphalt Ltd. The road overbridge is just visible behind the wooden fencing and the house to the left still stands. *Chris Gammell/TG*

WORTHY DOWN HALT was a bleak and uninspiring place at which to alight, particularly in winter. It is referred to on the 1-inch Ordnance Survey Map as 'Worthy Down Platform', which shows it almost at the end of a road apparently leading to nowhere. In fact the road led to a military establishment, hence the need for the halt, which was opened in 1918. The photograph again dates from December 1959.

In 1993 the old platform is still to be found amongst the trees and the trackbed is used as a footpath. The entrance to the halt from the nearby road overbridge still exists, although overgrown. *Chris Gammell/TG*

**KINGS WORTHY** was another decrepit station, still open when this photograph was taken. The station was built in 1909, 18 years after the line itself was opened.

The station has been completely obliterated and the site is now under the A34 road; a visit on summer Saturdays is not recommended as the constant stream of cars precludes photography and is also dangerous! The site of the goods yard seen in the right distance of the 'past' photograph is where the roofs of the modern buildings are located in front of the row of houses. *Chris Gammell/TG*

WINCHESTER CHESIL occupied a cramped location immediately beyond a tunnel under St Giles Hill on the eastern side of the city; the tunnel portal is just visible beyond the train, and the station fitted between this and the footbridge. The line then continued south by skirting the city and meeting the LSWR Bournemouth main line at Shawford Junction (see page 52). Class 'E1' No 31067 leaves Chesil on a special train from London Bridge to Eastleigh via Newbury on 22 May 1960. Between 1958 and 1961 a DMU service was run on summer Saturdays between Southampton and Winchester Chesil to relieve pressure at Winchester City station. Winchester Chesil to Shawford Junction was closed completely in April 1966.

This is the view on 3 April 1993. The trackbed has become a road and the station site is occupied by a multi-storey car park. The footbridge is still in use, although it has been rebuilt. *Both TG*

# INDEX OF LOCATIONS